12 GREAT TIPS ON
WRITING FICTION

by Catherine Elisabeth Shipp

STORY LIBRARY

www.12StoryLibrary.com

12-Story Library is an imprint of Peterson Publishing Company and Press Room Editions.

Produced for 12-Story Library by Red Line Editorial

Photographs ©: alphaspirit/Shutterstock Images, cover, 1; PR Newswire/AP Images, 4; Igor Golovniov/ Shutterstock Images, 5, 28; LifesizeImages/iStockphoto, 6; Ollyy/Shutterstock Images, 7; Art Konovalov/Shutterstock Images, 8; Oksana Shufrych/Shutterstock Images, 9; Steve Debenport/ iStockphoto, 11; Bill Florence/Shutterstock Images, 12; Npeter/Shutterstock Images, 14; Castleski/ Shutterstock Images, 15; Monkey Business Images/Shutterstock Images, 16; Stokkete/Shutterstock Images, 17; Zanariah Salam/Shutterstock Images, 18; Brendan Howard/Shutterstock Images, 19; LifetimeStock/Shutterstock Images, 20; Sara Placey/iStock/Thinkstock, 21; Vereshchagin Dmitry/ Shutterstock Images, 23; Thinkstock, 25, 29; Ermolaev Alexander/Shutterstock Images, 26; Pixsooz/ Shutterstock Images, 27

Library of Congress Cataloging-in-Publication Data
Names: Shipp, Catherine Elisabeth, 1969- author.
Title: 12 great tips on writing fiction / by Catherine Elisabeth Shipp.
Other titles: Twelve great tips on writing fiction
Description: Mankato, MN : 12-Story Library, 2017. | Series: Great tips on
    writing | Includes bibliographical references and index.
Identifiers: LCCN 2016002321 (print) | LCCN 2016004534 (ebook) | ISBN
    9781632352743 (library bound : alk. paper) | ISBN 9781632353245 (pbk. :
    alk. paper) | ISBN 9781621434429 (hosted ebook)
Subjects: LCSH: Fiction--Authorship--Juvenile literature.
Classification: LCC PN3355 .S55 2016 (print) | LCC PN3355 (ebook) | DDC
    808.3--dc23
LC record available at http://lccn.loc.gov/2016002321

Printed in the United States of America
Mankato, MN
May, 2016

Access free, up-to-date content on this topic plus a full digital version of this book. Scan the QR code on page 31 or use your school's login at 12StoryLibrary.com.

Table of Contents

Choose Realistic or Otherworldly

Writing fiction is an amazing way to tell stories. It lets you dig into your imagination. You can create characters, settings, and dialogue. It's your chance to make things up and not get in trouble.

Fiction tells stories that are not real. One type of fiction is realistic fiction. It is exactly that: stories that could really happen. Realistic fiction includes Gary Paulsen's *Hatchet*, Beverly Cleary's *Ramona the Pest*, and Kate DiCamillo's *The Tiger Rising*. All of these stories could actually happen in real life. Realistic fiction does not have magic or anything supernatural.

One genre of realistic fiction is historical fiction. Historical fiction could also happen in real life. But the story usually takes place in the past. For example, *Little House on the Prairie* by Laura Ingalls Wilder happens in the 1870s. The characters are from Wilder's real life. But the author made up details such as the dialogue.

Otherworldly fiction is different from realistic fiction. Otherworldly

The Lion, the Witch, and the Wardrobe includes a talking lion.

Quick Tips

- Fictional stories are at least partly made up.
- Decide what type of fiction you want to write.
- If you write realistic fiction, make sure it could happen in real life.

fiction includes science fiction, fantasy, and traditional stories. These stories could not really happen. An example of science fiction is *A Wrinkle in Time* by Madeleine L'Engle. In this book, the main character has to rescue her dad from another planet. Fantasy stories often have magical or supernatural elements. An example is *The Lion, the Witch, and the Wardrobe* by C. S. Lewis. The wardrobe, or clothes closet, leads four young siblings to another world where animals can talk. Traditional stories include fairy tales, fables, and myths. An example is *The Three Little Pigs.*

DIFFERENT WORLDS

The following is an example of realistic fiction:

Dana loved to dance. She twirled. She leaped. She tapped. Dana danced through dinner. She danced through dessert. Finally, her mom stopped her spinning, sat Dana down, and said, "Please eat."

Compare it to an example of otherworldly fiction:

Dana loved to dance. She twirled with flowers. She leaped over houses. She tapped all the way over the rainbow. Dana danced until her mom stopped her. "Please eat," her mom said. "Your tap shoes want to take a nap."

Pigs build houses in *The Three Little Pigs.*

2

Use Your Personal Experience to Your Advantage

Fiction means the story is pretend. But you can use some real memories to help give you ideas. Mixing what you know with what you make up can build a stronger fictional story. You can ask family members about when you were young. You can look at pictures. You can even use things that happened to your family and friends, but check with them first.

> Real memories can be the start of your fictional story.

Imagine a tornado siren sounded off when you were little. Your parents told you they took you to the basement. They took a radio. You all stayed down there for about an hour. Nothing happened to your home or town, but a tornado hit a

Characters might be able to fly in otherworldly stories.

town close by. If you write a realistic fiction story, you can use your experience and add made-up details. You could write about parents and a young child. Your dialogue will be made up. The setting can be a pretend place.

If you write an otherworldly story, you can add magical or supernatural things. Maybe the young child can fly and sees the tornado coming. She warns her parents. Maybe the parents have magical powers and can stop the tornado from destroying the town.

Whichever memories you use, make sure to include all five senses. Your five senses are sight, sound, smell,

touch, and taste. Sight is often the sense used most. But what did the tornado sound like? What did the basement smell like? Did the flying child touch the tornado? Was the family hungry? Use your five senses to write strong descriptions in your story.

Quick Tips

- Use your memories to help build a fictional story.
- Use others' experiences to help build a story, either realistic or otherworldly.
- Always include all five senses to add details to your writing.

3

Avoid Using Clichés

Figurative language is used to express something beyond the literal or exact meaning. It helps readers think about things in new ways. Examples include similes and metaphors.

When you use the words *like* or *as* to compare two unlike things, it's called a simile. An example is, "Her bright-gold crown was like the sun." When you write a comparison without one of those words, it's called a metaphor. An example is, "The queen was a shining star, guiding her people through dark times."

A cliché is a saying that is used too often. It is not original. A cliché can be literal. This means the words carry their normal meaning. "Better safe than sorry" is a cliché that means just what it says: "Don't take chances."

Other clichés are figurative. This means they have secondary meanings. An example is, "When life gives you lemons, make lemonade." Literally, this means a person should make a recipe with a particular ingredient, in this case, lemonade from lemons. Lemons are sour, but lemonade is sweet. Figuratively,

The simile "like looking for a needle in a haystack" means the thing is almost impossible to find.

Quick Tips

- Avoid writing clichés in your stories.
- If you like the meaning of a particular cliché, rewrite it. Use original words.
- Use similes and metaphors to make your descriptions stronger.

then, this cliché means a person should find ways to be happy even if things are not going well.

As you write fiction, come up with your own original ideas and words. Even if you like a particular cliché, make it your own. Suppose you want to use the cliché "strong as an ox." This is a figurative way of saying someone is very strong. Instead of using the cliché, try different comparisons. For example, you could say, "He is as strong as a tugboat pulling a barge." Writing figurative language without using clichés will help readers think differently.

Sour and sweet can figuratively mean upset and happy.

4

Create Believable Characters

When you write fiction, you need believable characters. Even in otherworldly fiction, characters must be credible. Author E. M. Forster taught that characters fall into one of two categories: round and flat. Round characters are complicated. They change during the story. They are more real. They make mistakes or might surprise the reader. Flat characters are simple and do not change. They might be stereotypical instead of unique. They are also not as important in the story.

To create credible, round characters, it is important to include information about how a character is feeling. This comes through in what the character says and thinks. You, the writer, need to give this information to the reader. For example, let's

say a character named Brady tries out for football. He's the tallest and biggest player on the field. What

SHOWING EMOTION

Good writers show how their characters are feeling through actions. What emotions do these two examples show?

Emily trembled at the microphone. Ms. Holmblad gave her the word to spell. Emily's mom stared at her daughter. Her dad blurted out, "You get this word right!"

Emily stood at the microphone. Ms. Holmblad gave her the word to spell. Emily's mom crossed her fingers. Her dad mouthed the words, "No problem," and smiled at his daughter.

Flat characters' actions are predictable.

would make him a flat character? Being tough, being mean, and becoming the star bully. Maybe he says things that aren't smart. Those things would be stereotypical of a football player. What would make Brady a round character? He tells his mom he's nervous for tryouts. He's also the vice president of the chess club. He uses his chess skills to help the team work together.

In order to be credible, characters also need to act consistently. Author J. K. Rowling's fantasy series Harry Potter has many credible characters. One of the most unique is an elf named Dobby. He was unlike any character who appeared in her books. Dobby would suddenly appear and try to help Harry and his friends. But he also tried to hurt himself. He thought he was not being obedient to his true owners, the Malfoys. The reader knew that Dobby would always try to help Harry.

Quick Tips

- Make sure to include round, or complicated, characters.
- Write what your main character says or thinks.
- Include what other characters say or think about each other.
- Write characters who are unique and consistent.

5

Determine Your Unique Point of View

One of the most important features of your story is point of view, or who tells the story. There are several points of view from which you can tell your story.

The broadest point of view you can use is third person. This means you write using words such as *he* and *she*. There are different ways to write third-person narration. Your point of view can be omniscient, or all knowing. This means you can describe all of the characters' thoughts as well as their

actions. For example, if you write about a boy playing baseball, you can write his thoughts when he is up to bat. You can write what his teammates in the dugout and parents in the stands are thinking, too.

Another kind of third-person narration is the limited perspective. This means you focus on the thoughts and feelings of only one character. In this case, you can write about the boy's thoughts while he is playing

In third-person omniscient, you can write the thoughts of any of your characters.

FIRST OR THIRD PERSON

An example of first-person narration:

> I stepped to the plate. I gripped the bat tighter. Both of my feet dug into the dirt by home plate. I thought to myself, *I can do this. I can hit my first-ever homerun.*

Compare to third-person limited from the dad's point of view:

> The dad watched with pride as his son stepped to the plate. The boy gripped his bat tighter. Both of the boy's feet dug into the dirt by home plate. The dad wondered what was going through his son's head.

baseball. But you cannot write what others are thinking.

First-person point of view is different from third person. In first person, you write as though you are one of the characters. You use the words *I* and *we.*

When you write in third-person limited or in first person, you restrict how much information the reader has access to. Not giving the reader insight into every character can help the story have suspense. It can also allow you to include surprises in your story.

First and third person are used most often. But some writers use second person. This is when you use the word *you.* For example, "You step up to the plate. You grip the bat tighter. Both of your feet dig into the dirt by home plate. You tell yourself you can hit your first homerun."

Quick Tips

- When you write in third-person omniscient, use *he* or *she.* You can write what several characters think and feel.
- When you write in third-person limited, use *he* or *she.* You can write what only one character thinks and feels.
- When you write in first person, use *I* and *we.*

13

Where on Earth Is Your Setting?

All stories must take place somewhere. In realistic fiction, you can use real places. Your story could take place in Seattle, Washington. But your town, state, or country doesn't have to be real. For example, your story could take place in Frame Lake, Minnesota. There is no such town as Frame Lake in Minnesota. But Minnesota is real. Or maybe your story takes place in a country called Octobia. Octobia is not real. But your story still takes place on Earth. As long as the story includes things that could happen, you can write realistic fiction in made-up locations.

Stories also happen in a certain time. If you want to set your story in a year in the past, research some things that happened that year. Suppose your story takes place in 1969. An astronaut first walked on the moon in that year. Including real-life details such as this in your story will help make your story feel real to readers. On the other hand, the year 2136 has not yet arrived. You cannot write about this year in realistic fiction. But you can in otherworldly fiction.

Another thing to consider with

Realistic fiction does not need to take place in a real town or city on Earth.

Realistic fiction can take place in space as long as the events could happen.

setting is the season. Does your story take place in summer, fall, winter, or spring? If your story is otherworldly fiction, are there even seasons?

No matter which setting you pick, make sure to include details about it in your story. Using details is especially important if the setting is imaginary. You want readers to be able to see in their minds where the story takes place.

Quick Tips

- For realistic fiction, at least part of the location must be real.
- For otherworldly fiction, the setting can be made up.
- Pick a time and season for your story.
- Put details about your setting into your story.

TRY IT OUT

Write details about a real place. Now make up a setting that is otherworldly. Maybe it's another planet. Maybe it's underground. Write details about it.

Work Out the Right Style and Tone

When you write a story, you must figure out its style and tone. The style of a story is how the story is written. The two parts that help determine style are diction and syntax. Diction consists of the kinds of words you choose to write. For example, you can write, "The young lady received a new electronic device to commemorate her day of birth." This style is more formal. Or you can say, "The girl got a new laptop for her birthday." This is more informal. Depending on your characters, you may also write slang: "My sis got a cool new laptop."

Syntax is the way you build sentences. It can help the reader learn about the narrator. For example, a character might

Characters talking to friends might speak differently to each other than they do to a teacher.

speak in long sentences: "I need to take the dog for a walk, since he's been confined to the house all day." A different person may speak in short sentences or even fragments: "Taking the dog out. Cooped up all day."

The tone of your story is the feeling or mood it portrays to the reader. Tone often fits a particular emotion, such as sad, serious, or excited. For example, let's say you are writing a story about a police officer

Crime stories often have a dramatic tone.

investigating a crime. The tone will probably be serious. Make sure your story's tone stays the same. Changing it can be confusing to the reader and will make your story less believable.

DICTION, SYNTAX, AND TONE

This example shows an informal diction, a normal syntax, and a tone of excitement:

> Alex returned to the end of the line. The line was long once again. He kept leaning to the side, looking past the people to see if they'd moved closer. He couldn't wait! His friends had gone to a different ride. They didn't want to ride this rollercoaster for the tenth time. But Alex was ready to zoom once again!

Quick Tips

- Figure out how you want to write your words: formally, informally, or with slang. Different characters will use different word choices.
- Figure out how you want to build your sentences. Again, different characters will speak differently.
- Keep the tone of your story consistent.

Put Together a Powerful Plot

The plot of any story is the order in which it moves forward. Most stories have an introduction, a rising action, a turning point, a falling action, and a conclusion.

A good way to imagine the plot is to think of a roller coaster. After you get in the seat and buckle up, the cars move slowly to get to a hill. This part is the introduction. You introduce some of the main characters, the setting, and maybe even a conflict or problem. The hill is the rising action. This is when the main character is trying to achieve a goal. All the scenes show conflicts or problems. The character has a hard time achieving the goal. The

Good plots take readers on an exciting ride.

rising action is generally the longest part of a story.

The turning point is when it's decided if the character achieves his or her goal. This part is the top of the hill. It's often the most exciting part of the story. Sometimes, it's the saddest. The falling action comes after the turning point. This part is going down the big hill. It gives the readers answers to questions. The reader knows the story will end soon. The conclusion is the end of the story. The roller coaster pulls to a stop.

Many times, the plot is chronological. This means the action moves forward in time. Sometimes, the writer will include a flashback. A flashback is when a character remembers something that

The rising action is like the hill on a rollercoaster.

happened in the past. For example, in Kate DiCamillo's book *The Tiger Rising*, the main character, Rob, has a flashback. He remembers when he went to his mom's funeral six months earlier.

TRY IT OUT

Draw a plot line with all the parts: introduction, rising action (make this line longer), turning point, falling action, and conclusion. Use this to help plan your story.

Quick Tips

- Include an introduction, rising action, turning point, falling action, and conclusion.
- Make the turning point the most exciting or saddest part of your story.
- Write chronologically, unless you include a flashback.

Build Interesting Scenes

All stories are structured into scenes. What are scenes? Think about your day at school. You arrive, you turn in your homework, and you start your math lesson. Or maybe you go to phys ed or start reading time. Whatever the schedule, there is an order. Your schedule is like a block of scenes that tells the story of your day. Similarly, when you write, your story will be divided into different sections.

You can choose where you want your story to begin. If your story is about a fourth grader, you do not need to start at the beginning of the school year. Your first scene might take place when the character was in kindergarten. In the same way, your story does not need to end at the end of the school year. You can pick how much time your story covers.

Each scene in your story should have a beginning, a middle, and an end. In order to write a scene that has each of these characteristics, ask yourself three questions. What does the character want? What is stopping the character from getting it? And does the character get what he or she wants? For

Scenes make up a story like classes make up a school day.

Quick Tips

- Order your scenes in a way the reader can understand.
- Write each scene with a beginning, a middle, and an end.
- Make it difficult for your character to get what he or she wants.

TRY IT OUT

Create a character. Brainstorm a list of five things the character might want. Pick one. Now come up with a list of things that might stop the character from achieving the goal.

example, let's say a boy named Nick wants to swing on the swings at recess. Because it's an otherworldly story, an orange octopus sits on the swings. Its eight legs cover all eight swings. The octopus is stopping Nick from swinging. As the writer, you have to decide what happens. Does Nick talk to the octopus, and the octopus moves one leg for Nick to

swing? Or does the octopus refuse to move, and Nick walks away from the swings unhappy?

> Obstacles keep characters from achieving their goals.

21

Establish Conflict

Conflict is a part of life. Similarly, struggles and problems play a big role in fiction. They are what the main character has to work through during the course of the story. A writer can include conflict in fiction in many different ways.

There are two types of conflict: external and internal. External conflict is what happens to a character on the outside. This conflict can happen with another character or group of characters. Or it can be a conflict against the setting. For example, maybe your character's family is flying to New Hampshire for a wedding. But a snowstorm hits the airport in Detroit. The family is stuck. In this case, the weather is the source of conflict.

Internal conflict is what happens to a character inside his or her mind. This kind of conflict means the character is struggling with a decision or doubting something. For example, let's say a character named Elliot is a best friend to a boy named Bret. Bret steals a pack of gum from a store. Elliot wants to tell an adult, but he also doesn't want to get his best friend in trouble. Elliot's tough decision is an internal conflict.

Small conflicts may be solved at the end of a scene. For example, the snowstorm will eventually

TRY IT OUT

A character wants to run track, but she's afraid she'll be too slow. Write a scene in which she decides whether to go out for the team. What helps her make her decision?

Weather is a form of external conflict.

stop. Elliot will make a decision about Bret. These conflicts and solutions are part of the rising action. But the biggest conflict is decided at the turning point. What if Elliot made the choice to tell an adult? Maybe Bret never talked to Elliot again.

EXTERNAL AND INTERNAL

The girl in the following example has external conflict because her parents don't agree. She also has internal conflict. She doesn't know which sport to play:

Shae loved dance. She also loved hockey. Her mom wanted her to play hockey, but her dad wanted her to dance. Shae didn't know what to do. And she had only a week to decide which was best.

Quick Tips

- Include conflict in your stories to make them interesting.
- Use both internal and external conflicts.
- Small conflicts can be solved throughout the story.
- The big conflict is solved at the turning point.

Write Strong Dialogue

Characters think and act in particular ways in stories. Dialogue is a great place to show your characters' relationships. It tells the reader how two characters feel about each other. Some of the characters' inner thoughts come out. But writing dialogue is not just for developing your characters. Strong dialogue can also move the action of the book forward.

To make your dialogue strong, avoid small talk and presenting facts. For example, when two people meet each other, it's not usually necessary to write greetings. Also, never write just facts:

"Katie, you have light-brown hair and freckles," said Liza.

"You have glasses," said Katie.

A CONVERSATION

The dialogue between these two boys shows they are good friends:

The two boys sat on their bikes in front of the school.

"Sorry," said Matthew, "but you can't spend the night Friday."

"What?" said Aaron. "You promised like five times!"

"I know, but my grandma is moving in," said Matthew.

"Grandma Jackie? Why?"

"Because she fell a month ago and needs help doing stuff."

"Man, I really wanted to finish that 1,000-piece puzzle," said Aaron.

"Yeah, me, too. Hey, maybe you can come and she can help us!"

TRY IT OUT

Write a dialogue for three friends who can't agree on where to play. Now write one in which two of the three friends agree and the third doesn't.

Quick Tips

- Write dialogue that includes more than small talk or facts.
- Focus on information that is important to the story.
- For the dialogue tag, use *said* most of the time.

Instead, focus on the important exchange between characters:

"Oh, Liza," Katie said, "I heard something weird about Ms. Smith."

"What is it? Please tell me," Liza said. "I'll bring you a lollipop tomorrow."

In this example of dialogue, we learn that Katie knows a secret about her teacher. This advances the plot. We also learn that Liza is willing to bring Katie something to find out what it is. Without the dialogue saying so, we can guess they are good friends.

Another way to write strong dialogue is to not use distracting dialogue tags. Dialogue tags, such as "Liza said," help the reader keep track of who is speaking. New writers often try using words such as *growled* and *praised*. But writing *said* is usually best. The dialogue itself can show the speaker's emotion. Also, you do not need to use a dialogue tag if it's clear who is speaking.

Dialogue is a great way to reveal your characters' thoughts.

25

Revise until Your Story Shines

A good writer isn't done with a story when the first draft, or version, is written. A good writer isn't done when the second draft is written. Many authors edit or revise their work over and over again to make it stronger. There are many ways to revise a story.

A good writer reads the story all the way through and looks for things to improve. Imagine you are reading the story for the first time. Does everything make sense? Are there conflicts? Are the characters believable? Does it have the effect you hoped it would?

A good writer also reads the story out loud. Doing so can help you slow down and listen to the words. Did you forget any words? For example, "The boy took ladder out of the garage." The word *the* is missing. Did you add any extra words? For example, "Morgan said to never talk not to speak in the library." A few words need to be deleted. Did you repeat the same word in a sentence or paragraph

All writers should revise their work.

Revision helps you finish your work strong.

several times? For example, "The waterslide had water in the tubes, and you went into the water and fell into the water." Reading aloud will also let you listen to how the dialogue sounds. Does it sound natural? Fix any mistakes you find. Now is it ready? Not quite.

This may be hard to do, but put your story away for a while. Don't read it for a few days, a week, or even longer. When you read it again, it will be like a new story. Ask yourself the same questions: Does everything make sense? Does anything need to be fixed? Ask yourself different questions: Is your point of view consistent? Does your story show and not tell?

A final check could be for a different reader to read it. This could be a teacher or a parent or even a friend. Is there anything that confused them? What did they like? Do not be afraid to rewrite the story several times. You want to make it shine.

Quick Tips

- Read the story. Ask yourself questions such as, "Does it make sense?"
- Read the story out loud. Fix any mistakes.
- Put your story away for some time. Read it again and ask yourself the same questions.
- Have another reader read your story and give you feedback.
- Rewrite until your story shines.

Writer's Checklist

✓ Decide if you want to write realistic fiction or otherworldly fiction.

✓ Use your own memories to help yourself with story ideas.

✓ Avoid clichés in your writing. Be original with your words.

✓ Make your characters unique, believable, and consistent in their thoughts and actions.

✓ Decide on your point of view or who will narrate your story.

✓ Determine a place and a time when your story will be set.

✓ Pick a style and a tone for your fiction.

✓ Write scenes that include what a character wants. Also, write about why it's hard to reach this goal. At the end of the scene, tell if the character achieves the goal.

✓ Build your scenes into a plot. Include an introduction, a rising action, a turning point, a falling action, and a conclusion.

✓ Include external and internal conflict with your characters.

✓ Write scenes that Include important dialogue.

✓ Reread and revise your story to make it stronger.

Glossary

credible
Believable.

dialogue
A conversation between two or more characters.

flashback
A scene set in an earlier time than the main story.

formal
Following an established form or set of rules.

genre
A category of literature.

narration
The act of telling a story.

slang
Language that is very informal.

stereotypical
Not unique.

supernatural
Beyond our universe or something not real.

suspense
When the reader doesn't know what is going to happen.

For More Information

Books

Basher, Simon. *Basher Basics: Creative Writing*. New York: Kingfisher, 2013.

Benke, Karen. *Rip the Page!: Adventures in Creative Writing*. Boulder, CO: Shambhala Publications, Inc., 2010.

Pearson, Yvonne. *Rev Up Your Writing in Fictional Stories*. Mankato, MN: The Child's World, 2015.

Visit 12StoryLibrary.com

Scan the code or use your school's login at **12StoryLibrary.com** for recent updates about this topic and a full digital version of this book. Enjoy free access to:

- Digital ebook
- Breaking news updates
- Live content feeds
- Videos, interactive maps, and graphics
- Additional web resources

Note to educators: Visit 12StoryLibrary.com/register to sign up for free premium website access. Enjoy live content plus a full digital version of every 12-Story Library book you own for every student at your school.

Index

About the Author

Catherine Elisabeth Shipp is a writer and a teacher who has published more than a dozen children's books, with more on the way. She lives with her husband and twins in Minnesota.